The *COACHING ERA*

by
Geoffrey Body and Roy Gallop

GW00673715

Stage and mail coach travel
in and around
Bath, Bristol and Somerset

FIDUCIA PRESS   2003   KINGSMEAD PRESS

THE
COACHING
ERA

Stage and mail coach travel
in and around
Bath, Bristol and Somerset

by

Geoffrey Body and Roy Gallop

Design and typography
by
Roy Gallop and Ken Griffiths

Front cover: A Royal Mail coach on the route from London to Bath and Wells. Traditionally the coach left London at 8pm, ran overnight to Bath and then on via Wells, Taunton and Exeter to reach Devonport at 9.50pm on the second day.

Title page: A contemporary engraving by W H Pyne of a fully laden stagecoach.

Page 3: Chaise and four at full gallop under the urging of two postillions.

Rear cover: As the Britannia Inn, this was the Castle Cary calling point for the 'Red Rover' coach which linked Bristol and Weymouth on alternate days.

© Fiducia Press 2003 ISBN 0 946217 14 9
© Kingsmead Press 2003   ISBN 1 85026 019 2
in association with the Bath Postal Museum

CONTENTS

Published by Fiducia Press, 10 Fairfield Road, Bristol BS3 1LG
and Kingsmead Press, Globe House, East Moors Road, Cardiff CF24 5EE
Copyright Geoffrey Body and Roy Gallop.

Printed in Great Britain by Doveton Press Ltd., of Bristol.

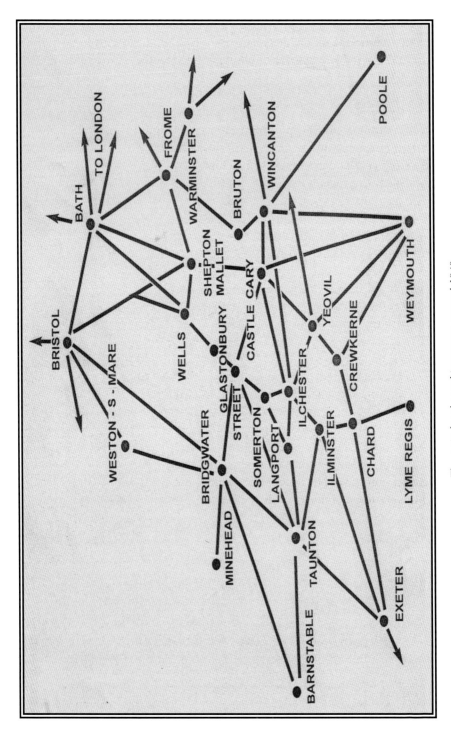

The main local coaching routes around 1840.

Dean Jonathan Swift (1667-1745), the author of *Gulliver's Travels,* frequently travelled to and from Ireland on horseback. However, on one occasion he used the stagecoach to Chester. He penned the following lines on the experience:

Roused from sound sleep - thrice called - at length I rise,
Yawning, stretch out my arms, half-closed my eyes;
By steps and lanthorn enter the machine,
And take my place, how cordially between
Two aged matrons of excessive bulk,
To mend the matter, too, of meaner folk;
While in like mood, jammed in on t'other side,
A bullying Captain and a fair one ride,
Foolish and fair, and in whose lap a boy-
Our plague eternal, but *her* only joy.
At last, the glorious number to complete,
Steps in my landlord for that bodkin seat;
When soon, by every hillock, rut, and stone,
In each other's faces by turn we're thrown.
This grandam scolds, *that* coughs, the Captain swears,
The fair one screams, and has a thousand fears;
While our plump landlord, trained in other lore,
Slumbers at ease, nor yet ashamed to snore;
And master Dicky, in mother's lap,
Squalling, at once brings up three meals of pap.
Sweet company! Next time, I do protest, Sir,
I'd walk to Dublin, ere I ride to Chester!

True to his word Swift never made another stagecoach journey!

AUTHORS' NOTE: *The care and comfort of coach travellers did steadily improve over the years but most advertisements for early coach services included the words 'if God permit' and prudent people might even have felt it wise to make a will before setting out on a journey! Add the discomforts of long journeys over poor roads in vehicles with hard seats and no springs to the hazzards of weather, breakdowns, bed bugs, footpads and a few drunken, reckless or repacious coachmen and one can understand Dean Swift's views.*

Although the coaching era is long past, traces do remain as is revealed by the above photographs. The stagecoach was used on the London to Falmouth route. The coaching inn yard is still in evidence at the Swan Hotel, Wells.

Journeys of Introduction

Records from the coaching era being somewhat sparse the preparation of this account has, of necessity, been based on a recipe of wholesome research ingredients with just a dash of surmise. Hopefully the latter will make the repast that little bit more tasty but the authors are, in any event, very ready to heed informed comment on their offering. That said, the tradition of a weighty introduction has been abandoned in favour of a few sample journeys designed to prepare the palate for what is to follow.

The 'Defiance' Dispute

The London-Exeter *Defiance* coach was put on in 1823 to compete with the well-established *Subscription Coach* service and may well have derived its name from that challenge. Both followed the route via Andover, Wincanton, Ilchester and Ilminster and both were scheduled to complete the 168-mile journey in 19 hours. The down direction *Defiance* left the Bull in London's Aldgate at 3.15pm daily and called at the Bull & Mouth in St Martin's-le-Grand before beginning the main portion of its journey at 3.45pm. Its rival set off from the latter just fifteen minutes later, surely a recipe for some exciting running by both!

On one occasion, however, the excitement took a rather different form and happened on the Somerset portion of the journey. For mile after mile following the original departure from Mrs Anne Nelson's Bull Inn the journey had been much as usual but this changed dramatically as the coach approached a turnpike gate on the Ilchester Trust's pre-A303 route. As usual, the guard blew his horn to warn of their approach but his mate on the box found that the gate had not been opened and had to apply the brakes in a hurry. It seems that the toll keeper was in arrears with his monthly payments to the turnpike trust and they had asked the coach proprietor to make his usual weekly payment direct to them instead of at the gate. The gate keeper was having none of this and, after some angry words, insisted on being paid three shillings before he would let the coach pass.

Not content with one victory the pikekeeper then used a horse and trap to dash to

With a straight left to the tollgate keeper's jaw the guard of the 'Defiance' reinforces his argument for having the tollgate opened for his coach and passengers. Even the horses watch with interest.

the next gate and ensure solidarity in the dispute by having the passage of the coach barred there too. Not surprisingly, this incensed the poor coach guard who rightly felt himself an innocent victim in this dispute. To have done with the nonsense he went to the toolbox that most coaches carried and attacked the barrier with a crowbar, an action that, in its turn, proved too much for the gatekeeper. As the chronicler puts it, 'This led to fisticuffs between himself (the guard) and the keeper, in which the keeper came off second best. The bout ended in the gate's being opened.'

8

Parson Holland's Complaints

Born in 1746, William Holland became vicar of Overstowey at the age of 43. Sadly William, and Mary his wife, lost four children to an outbreak of scarlet fever in 1795. Two years later their pain was eased a little when 47-year old Mary gave birth to a son who they named after his father. When he reached the age of twelve a decision was taken to send young William to a school in London then being run by his former master from Bridgwater. Not unnaturally, William and Mary were anxious about their son's impending travel adventure, especially as snow began to fall on the day before the journey was to take place.

The 12-year old Holland lad was booked to travel on Fromont's coach leaving Bridgwater at 3am on the morning of Sunday 15 January 1809. His mother had taken him to an inn at Bridgwater and someone had been paid to keep an eye on him until journey time. By all accounts the lad behaved well, was civil to his companions at breakfast and took up his inside seat in the coach in the best of spirits.

At the very last moment before departure another intending passenger arrived and claimed the seat that William was occupying. With or without his consent the boy was forced to surrender its relative comfort and manage as best he could in the basket where the luggage was carried. He must have been bruised, dispirited and near-frozen by the time the coach reached Wells and there was room for him to be taken back inside. Parson Holland was furious at what he called a 'cruel and brutal' act. Not sure whether to blame the book-keeper or the coachman he wrote a strongly-worded letter to the coach proprietor. What answer he got we do not know but the fact that his son's luggage also got lost cannot have helped matters!

Clergyman Holland seems to have had a rather poor opinion of transport providers. His horseback journeys seem to have gone well enough but his diaries do record a suspicion that the mail coach men were selling off his daily paper on the journey down from London. He also remarks that the Old Down Inn, hub of many local coach journeys and mail arrangements, did not impress him as much as it did other people. Arriving there after dark by post chaise in 1810 he had to complain about the 'dull little room' allocated to him. He was given a better one but still felt that the service was bad and the charges high.

Post 'Chase'

Posting inns, posting houses and similar establishments not only provided the fresh horses required at intervals along the stage and mail coach routes but also offered mounts for individual riders and a package of post chaise vehicle, horses and post boy or man to act as the postillion. These services originated with the provision of fresh mounts for the riders who provided the first postal services and then expanded as the network of coach services increased. The middle classes hired post chaises extensively to undertake journeys off the main coach routes or to connect with them.

The sub-title spelling is appropriate for a journey made in 1774 by the Reverend James Woodforde, for, despite paying a porter one shilling for a 6am call and for carrying his luggage to the Cross Inn in Oxford, he still missed the Bath coach which had left promptly at seven. Not to be beaten Woodforde hired a post chaise, gave chase and caught the coach up about five miles along its journey. Failing to get up until half an hour after his early call had cost the Reverend four shillings for the hire plus a shilling for the driver.

Another example of a post chaise journey is the one made by Solomon Franklin, a steward to the Trevellyan estate at Nettlecombe. This was in 1777, about the time Jenner started gathering evidence about tackling smallpox by means of cow-pox vaccination. Other surgeons were using small infections of the disease as a way of preventing something worse and Franklin hired a post chaise to take the Trevellyan lads, William and Edward, to Bristol 'to be enoculated', presumably against the risk of smallpox which was greatly feared at that period. His account book records the expenses of the journey, including £2. 14s for chaise hire, 6/- for the driver and another 4/- spent on hay and corn at Bridgwater. 'Servants eating and beer going up' cost Franklin 13/9 with various other sums spent on provisions. Among the latter were 'oringes', doubtless brought by ship up river to Bridgwater, which cost 3/6. By travelling via Watchet the Trevellyan route would have been turnpiked since 1765 and have meant paying out several more shillings in tolls but the exact sum is not recorded.

The Rev. Woodforde's journey combination of post chaise and stage coach was an accident but another clergyman's use of private and public coaches for his journey was more calculated. On 1 April 1766 the Reverend Penrose, his wife and daughter and their manservant George set off in their own chaise from their home near Falmouth intent on a journey to Bath would occupy seven days and leave them somewhat the worse for wear.

The first day's journey went well enough, probably because the roads were kept in a reasonable condition in order to carry forward the American mail which the Navy's packet brigs landed at Falmouth. The Penrose horses were 'baited' and the travellers themselves refreshed at Grampound before going on to Lostwithiel and a supper of veal cutlets at the inn there. Hot rolls and tea got the party on the road again by half past seven the following morning and, despite one stop and some uncertainty about the route over Bodmin Moor, they were with their friends at Trebartha, high up the Lynher River, six hours later. This time they dined on a choice of beef, mutton, hog's pudding and fried oysters. This pattern continued as the Penrose group journeyed on to Okehampton and then to Exeter but they were already feeling the rigours of the journey. Everyone's bones ached and Mr Penrose was so stiff he could hardly get into and out of the chaise. Four miles beyond the cathedral city they spent two nights with friends, again enjoying some fine meals, and then set out to catch the Bath coach at Cullompton, glad they had used their own coach to spare the Reverend Penrose the early start that going to Exeter would

A stylised treatment of the coaching scene depicting a pleasant country inn with patient horses, a jolly crowd to see the excited travellers off and a jug of ale to sustain the coachman on his journey; or, perhaps lull him to sleep and a fall from his box! Not all stops were relaxed as this.

have entailed. He was now so unwell that he had to be lifted into the new vehicle, after which George was freed to return the horses to their starting point.

In the hands of a professional coach operator the journey on through Somerset went quite well. Our travellers declared the carriage 'easy' and the invalid found that having an apothecary as a travelling companion 'usefull (sic) on the road.' He managed, with further help, to take dinner at Taunton and spend the night at

Bridgwater. There was no stop in Wells, the coach continuing on to the busy inn at Old Down where dinner was taken before the final stretch into Bath. A sedan chair conveyed Mr Penrose to 'handsome lodgings' in Abbey Green to bring to a conclusion a 180-mile marathon of bruising travel only partly compensated by meeting many friends and dining rather well in their company.

The Early Years

In medieval England ordinary people did not travel much. Unless you were a retainer in the service of some rich nobleman, merchant or cleric your journeys would probably not extend beyond an occasional trip to and from the local market. Such outings would either be made on foot, in a farm cart, or on the back of a working horse or mule.

Exceptions included itinerant priests, pilgrims and chapmen but they, too, would normally have made their journeys on foot. The roads were hardly suitable for anything else since only the Church and a few of the more enterprising or enlightened landowners cared for the bridges, ferries and more important routes. Signs of better times began to emerge when an Act of 1555 put the responsibility for road maintenance squarely on the parish through which it ran and Elizabeth I set the fashion for using a coach of sorts as an alternative to riding on horseback or in a litter.

Stimulated by increasing trade and by somewhat patchy improvements in the road system the old reliance on packhorses for moving merchandise was supplemented by movement in long waggons from around the 1560s. Soon these were also carrying up to twenty passengers over 'stages' of the journey, admittedly in serious discomfort as seating was not provided. The daily or mileage charges were still beyond most ordinary people but the number of regular waggon services had risen to 200 by 1637. At the same time the wealthy were demanding a quicker journey than they could make by coastal vessel and a more comfortable one than riding a horse or using the clumsy coaches of the time. Ultimately these factors of better roads, the increasing demand for movement and improvements in vehicle design were to usher in the remarkable stage coach era.

One other major contribution to this process occurred in 1629 when the postal system previously used for government and other official mail was reorganised and began to accept private letters. On main roads this increased volume of mail was carried by mounted post-boys who were provided with accommodation and fresh horses at strategic inns along their route. The same facilities were also used to offer an official ancillary service which hired out horses and guides for private individuals who wished to travel on these main roads. The product of these various strands of evolution was to be the emergence in the middle of the 17th century of a public service of regular, timetabled coaches which was to last for two hundred years.

Coach services to the West featured in an advertisement dated 8 April 1658 which drew attention to a 2-day journey available to Salisbury on Mondays, Wednesdays and Fridays at a fare of 20/-. Getting to Exeter took twice as long and cost twice as much.

Fifteen years later the 4-day journey to Exeter still cost 40/- but the 6-horse coach took 6 days for the journey in winter and 45/- was then charged. Bristol got its first public coach service in 1660 or 1661. It only ran in the summer and meant three long days of travelling, each covering about 40 miles. The first English turnpike Act was then passed in 1663, a year in which Jerrat Gore's coach began a Bristol-London service for 25/- and the Bristol alderman William Colston was injured when his private coach overturned. The first coaches from Taunton began around 1675.

In 1667 London bill posters began to appear announcing:-

Flying Machine

All those desirous to pass from London to Bath,
or any other Place on their Road, let them repair
to the Bell Savage on Ludgate Hill and the
White Lion at Bath, at both which places they may
be received in a Stage Coach every Monday,
Wednesday and Friday, which performs the whole
journey in Three Days (if God permit), and sets forth
at five in the Morning.
Passengers to pay One Pound five Shillings each,
who are allowed to carry fourteen Pounds Weight -
for all above to pay three halfpence per pound.

Despite a starting time of 5am there were plenty of interested spectators to witness this pioneering event.

Not everyone approved of the growth in stage coach activity. A pamphlet of the time protested:-

'Formerly every man that had occasion to travel many journeys yearly or to ride up and down, kept horses for himself and servants, and seldom rid without one or two men; but now since every man can have a passage into every place he is to travel into, or to some place within a few miles of that part he designs to go unto they have left keeping of horses, and travel without servants; and York, Chester and Exeter stage-coaches, each of them with forty horses a-piece, carry eighteen passengers a week from London to either of these places, and, in like manner, as many in return from these places to London; which come in the whole to one thousand, eight hundred and seventy-two in the year. Now take it for granted that all that are carried from London to those places are the same that are brought back, yet are there nine hundred and thirty-six passengers carried by forty horses; whereas, were it not for these coaches, at least five hundred horses would be required to perform this work. These coaches and caravans hinder the consumption of all sorts of provisions for man and beast, thereby bringing down the rents

of lands. For instance, a coach with four horses carries six passengers, a caravan with four or five horses carries twenty or twenty-five. These, when they come to their inn, club together for a dish or two of meat, and, having no servants with them, spend not above twelve-pence or sixteen-pence a-piece at a place; yet perhaps use four, five or six pairs of sheets. Horses they have none but what draw them; and for those the coachmen agree with the innkeeper beforehand to have their hay and oats at so low a rate that he loseth by them, and is forced to beat down the price of them in the market, yet must let the coachman have them for what he pleaseth otherwise he carries his passengers to other inns; by which means the innholders get little or nothing, cannot pay their rent nor hold their inns, without great abatement. Two-third parts of what they formerly paid is, in some places, abated. Upon such accounts as these, innholders, where these coaches do come are undone; and if so, since most travellers travel in coaches, what must become of all the rest of the inns on the roads where the coaches stay not? Believe it, they are a considerable number, take all the grand roads in England, as York, Exeter, Chester, &c. There are about five hundred inns on each road, and those coaches do not call at but fifteen or sixteen of them; then what must follow, but that the rest be undone, and their landlords lose their rents?'

Fortunately for the coming generations of travellers and for the growth and economic wellbeing of the country this gloomy outlook proved totally unfounded. Certainly, as journeys got quicker some inns would be passed by and lose their livelihood but others were opened at the new calling points which in some cases became the nucleus of new communities. More travel also stimulated more business and more employment resulting in the benefits of additional coach services extending to a whole range of ancillary activities from a growing coach-building industry to the services of ostlers, farriers, porters and others needed to care for the coaches and their passengers.

Expansion in the 18th Century

A good omen of better things to come for road travel in the area around Somerset was the establishment of its first turnpike trust, the Bath Trust, in 1707. The Bristol Trust was then set up in 1727, with the Bridgwater Trust following in 1730. Starting with the most heavily used roads in their area these trusts took over responsibility from the parishes, providing improved road surfaces and maintaining them with money from the tolls levied on the users. The improvements were slow and, initially, not significant in terms of total mileage but they affected the most important routes and represented the beginnings of a transformation that would eventually relegate the old parish system and its reliance on unskilled surveyors and unwilling labour to the least important parts of the growing road network.

The improvements in transport as a whole were slow in the first half of the 18th century. In 1720 it still took four days to get from London to Exeter, each day starting at 3am and involving twelve gruelling hours on the road. Turnpikes in Devon and Cornwall were late in coming so any onward journey west from Exeter might be even worse. In 1729 a summer coach service began running between Bath and Exeter, northbound on Mondays, taking two and a half days on the journey including an overnight stop at Taunton, and returning from Bath every Thursday. The fare was one guinea, a lot of money at that period, but at least the facility existed. Ten years later a traveller from Frome to London would still have no choice but to endure a three day marathon by the 'old standing constant Frome flying waggon' and pay a similar sort of price for three days of springless jolting on top of a lumbering broad-wheeled vehicle dedicated primarily to goods conveyance.

On the London-Bath-Bristol route the first 'flying' coaches improved the journey time to two days early in the new century but that was then to remain the norm for some fifty years. The number of services did rise to three a week but they took from a 2am start until the late evening of the next day. By 1735 a coach was leaving James Wimble's Lamb Inn in Broadmead Bristol every Wednesday and Friday to carry travellers to Thomas How's Golden Heart at Gloucester. Its passengers could 'meet and dine' with those travelling in the opposite direction at the Red

Lyon (sic) at Newport.

Nationally the 10 new turnpike Acts passed in the first decade of the 18th century rose to 22 in the next and 46 in the 1720s, and by 1750 most of the major through routes in England had been turnpiked. The expansion continued throughout the century and by 1830 some 20,000 miles of road, some 10% of the total, had been turnpiked. In 1752 Somerset witnessed the establishment of the Taunton Trust with Yeovil, Wells and Shepton Mallet setting up in the following year. The full coaching era had yet to arrive but a much wider range of journeys was now available by combining coach travel with the hire of a post chaise for the less well-travelled portion. There is evidence, too, that some regular post chaise services were also operated, including one from Taunton to Ilminster established in 1752.

Although passage through a 'pike', or tollgate, would cost each 4-horse coach at least fourpence, the turnpike trusts brought not only better roads but also provided things like this milepost on the Bridgwater Trust's northbound route through Huntspill. (It would have been immensely valuable as a point of reference in the case of bad weather or breakdown.)

From the 1760s the pace of overall change seemed to speed up as did that of individual journeys. By 1764 a 2-day service was available between London and Exeter and by the following year Bristol people could get to Birmingham for 18/- by rising early enough to leave the Lamb at 4am and spend the night at Worcester before completing their journey by noon on the second day. In the opposite direction they could, on Mondays from 30 March 1767, leave the George Inn, 'without Temple Gate' at 5am and travel to Bridgwater for 10/-, to Taunton for 12/6d or to Exeter for £1 . 1s. In addition to luggage, goods were 'carried on reasonable terms.' Frome, too, was enjoying an alternative to the traditional waggon service with a 'flying coach' leaving for London three days a week and getting there in the sixteen hours between 7am and 11pm. Feeder services were also laid on as a contemporary advertisement shows:-

The Proprietors of the Frome Stage Machine In order to make it more agreeable *to their Friends in the West, have engaged to set out Post Chaises from the Christopher Inn in Wells every Sunday, Tuesday, and Thursday evenings, at Five o'clock, to stop at the George Inn, Shepton Mallett, and set out from thence at a quarter past six, to carry passengers and parcels to Frome, to be forwarded from thence to London in the One Day Flying Machine, which began on Sunday, April 12th, 1767: Also a chaise from Frome every Tuesday, Thursday, and Saturday evenings, to Shepton and Wells as soon as the Coach arrives from London.'*

For a period from 1765 we have more details of local road journeys thanks to the Reverend James Woodforde and his 'Diaries of a Country Parson 1758-1802'. Born in 1740 at Ansford, where his father was rector, young James was elected a scholar at New College, Oxford when he was nineteen and returned to Somerset in 1763 having been ordained a deacon and with a BA degree. He was very representative of the travelling middle classes.

Woodforde made his local journeys on horseback at home and while up at Oxford but records a coach trip back to Ansford after a visit to the former in 1765, using the coach via Burford, Cirencester and Tetbury to Bath. On top of the 9/- advance payment on his coach fare, the minister had to pay 10/6d for his excess luggage, 6d for a wake up call at 3am and then 1/6d for having his portmanteau carried to the coach starting point. Breakfast was taken at Burford where the balance of the fare was paid, and there was more to pay out for dinner and drinks during the stop at Tetbury. Arriving at Bath, Woodforde then supped and spent the night at the King's Arms in Broad Street before completing the journey to Ansford using a horse sent over by his father.

For the journeys for which no coach service was available, those who could afford it used a post chaise. This was how Woodforde journeyed to Bridgwater for an election rally in 1767. For the first stage he used a post chaise hired from the Ansford Inn which took him to Pipers Inn, Ashcott where another vehicle was then hired to take him to Catcott for an overnight stay with friends. The Pipers Inn post chaise continued its journey to Bridgwater on the second day, was stabled at the Globe Inn overnight and then used for the first stage of the return journey on the next day, its driver the better off by a 2/6d tip, the same amount that Woodforde won at whist that evening. This way of travelling was much more flexible and not excessively expensive. The charge for Ansford to Old Down and Old Down to Bath journeys remained at 10/6d for several years while a 1774 journey from Oxford to Ansford using hired post chaises all the way cost only £4 . 8s for the vehicles, all meals, tips and turnpikes.

In the 1770s, despite the country as a whole having over 500 turnpikes, Taunton was still served only by its London coach and the calls by the Bath to Exeter and Bristol to Exeter coaches. This was part of a pattern which saw the first coach operations concentrated on the traditional strategic routes from London, particularly as these offered the best traffic prospects for the emerging breed of professional coach operators. A decade on and the whole picture was to alter dramatically with the introduction of the first mail coaches.

The biggest change in road travel in the whole of the 18th century was the brainchild of Bath theatre manager John Palmer. He took as his starting point the numerous shortcomings of the existing Post Office system based on the use of mounted post-boys plus the occasional mail cart on busier routes. Ralph Allen, another Bath man, had already been instrumental in expanding the system by means of cross posts to connect with the main routes but poor punctuality and no small number of irregularities had remained a barrier to any significant improvement in either the quality or profitability of the postal services. A Post Office profit of £100,889 in 1727 was not matched again until 1764. Helped by Palmer's innovations from 1784 plus higher rates the profit figure went over the half million mark in 1797 and by 1806 had risen to £1,119,419.

The changes put forward by Palmer were simple in concept but radical in effect. His plan, resisted steadfastly by the Post Office until he won Prime Minister Pitt's support, was based upon the introduction of mail carriages which would carry letters, parcels and passengers, operate to a strict timetable and be provided with the security of an armed guard. The services would have absolute right of passage, pay no tolls and be controlled by stringent documentation of each journey stage and of the cargo carried.

Palmer never quite got rid of some antagonism within the Post Office bureaucracy but the first of his new mail coaches was put on the road in 1784 and immediately set a new standard with an average speed of nearly seven miles an hour between London and Bristol. This dramatic journey began at the Rummer in Bristol when a coach hired from Fromont of Thatcham set off for London at 4pm on 2 August. After calling at the Three Tuns in Bath and leaving there at 5.30pm it continued overnight to reach the Swan with Two Necks in Lad Lane at 8am. A new era was dawning.

Palmer's reward was his appointment as Controller General of the Post Office in 1786 by which time twenty of the new Royal Mail coaches were leaving London each evening with another seven routes linking provincial cities. One of the new services, introduced in 1785, was a route from London to Exeter via Bath, Wells and Taunton.

The introduction of mail coaches proved a wake-up call to operators of conventional stage coach services. In the middle of 1786 Woodforde records a journey from London to Bath in which he travelled by an overnight 'baloon' (sic) coach, so-called 'on Account of it travelling so fast, making it a point to be before the Mail Coach.' This service left London at 6.45pm with a light load of four passengers plus a guard on top and pulled by two fast horses. The advance fare was a guinea with another 9/- to pay en route. A 1787 notice regarding a three times a week service from Oxford to the White Hart at Bath also reveals another dimension, that of coach connections, by linking at Bath with Salisbury, Southampton, Weymouth, Exeter and Bristol coaches and at Exeter with those to Falmouth, Plymouth and Barnstaple. In 1790 Taunton also had a quicker service from London with departures every Monday, Wednesday and Friday at 4am and an arrival in Taunton on the evening of the following day. This service ran overnight in the summer months.

Bridgwater was well blessed with inns catering for coach, waggon and shipping business. Its steady growth led to the building of the Royal Clarence Hotel in the heart of the town in1825.

Despite the shortcomings of data collection at the time, directories around the year 1794 give a broad picture of coach services in Somerset as the 18th century neared its close. The main towns and those on the main routes were quite well served but places like Wellington, and Shepton Mallet had to rely on 'wagons and carts'. The Minehead entry averred that 'There is no road that way for carriages, therefore no mail, stage-coach or wagon sets out from thence' and the town had to rely on 'common stage carts' to Bristol, Taunton and Tiverton. As the Minehead United Trust had been established since 1765 this might be a commentary on the reliability of the information in early directories.

At Taunton the prestige service was apparently the mail coach from Exeter which arrived at the London Inn at 8.30am and set out again an hour later for London. Every day of the week it went on via Glastonbury to call at Wells around noon and depart again at 1pm. An hour later the down service left the cathedral city to arrive in Taunton at 6pm and then go forward to Exeter at half past. Meanwhile those travelling to London on Whitmarsh's 'new long coach' had been on the road since 4am, this service operating via Ilminster on Mondays, Wednesdays and Fridays with the balancing service getting back to Taunton at 8pm on Tuesdays, Thursdays and Saturdays. There seems also to have been a 'post coach' to London on the same days and carrying four passengers inside and one on the outside

Taunton was also served by the Bristol - Exeter route on which travellers had the choice of using a 'light coach', a diligence or Tomlin's caravan. The light coach left at 10am northbound every day except Sunday with the inwards working arriving at 1pm and going on to Exeter at 2pm. Calls were made at Bridgwater around noon. On Wednesdays and Fridays anyone journeying from Bristol to Barnstaple could catch the 5pm coach westwards from Taunton. The return workings from Barnstaple were on Thursdays and Sundays and got back into Taunton at 7pm.

The mail coach left Bridgwater for London at 10am and for Exeter at 2pm. Chard and Crewkerne were served by the *Royal Clarence* on its way from the Half Moon at Exeter to the Bull & Crown, Holborn. This coach called at the Red Lion, Chard for its passengers to take breakfast on Mondays, Wednesdays and Fridays with the down service stopping there in the afternoon on the alternate days. Wells had the same sort of three days a week service from the Christopher Inn to Bath, and Frome had a two days a week Bath service from the George. The Frome - London coach left the same inn at 3pm on Sundays, Tuesdays and Thursdays and got back at 10pm Tuesdays, Thursdays and Saturdays. The single fare was 27/-.

By using a horse or adding in the option of the private hire of a post chaise for part of the journey most travel permutations were possible at this period. The south eastern part of the county could, for example, connect at Salisbury with the London coach. Parson Woodforde did this in 1786, the journey from Cole to Salisbury costing him £2. Setting out in a chaise hired in Bruton, he used another one from Mere but could not get a third at Hindon where both he and Prime Minister Pitt found that all the horses were engaged, forcing him to 'bait horses' and continue with the same chaise all the way to Salisbury. After a day of exploring Salisbury and a night at the White Hart there he caught the 5am London coach and arrived in the capital at 6pm.

Although so much had been achieved since the days of the few unpredictable and uncomfortable coach services operating in the early years there were still many difficulties facing the coach operators and their clients, as will be clear from later chapters. Among the less dramatic of these were the taxes levied on passenger road vehicles as successive governments got the hang of taxing any essential or successful activity to pay for wars and other crises. The Trevellyan steward's account book records 'Duty on coach wheels' of £4 in 1776 rising to £5 in the following year. From 1783 duty of a half-penny had to be paid on every mile run and this was doubled two years later. As a result 'The Proprietors of the LONDON and TAUNTON COACH' were forced to:-

> *'respectfully inform the public that the Mile Duty on Stage-Coaches, by a late Act of Parliament, being doubled they are under the necessity of making a small advance in their fares.....'.*

Operators and Operations

The Coach Operators

Most coach operators were also innkeepers although some of the later services were based on investment partnerships, especially where local gentry needed a new route for their own convenience. When the *Defiance* coach began running between Exeter and London in April 1823 one of its backers was Ilminster magistrate William Hanning, despite the fact that this very same gentleman had supported the introduction of the *Subscription Coach* service eleven years earlier. Perhaps the latter had not lived up to his expectations. Even so the new service did not meet with universal approbation and was said to have 'started on the Sunday afternoon amid the shouts and imprecations of guards, coachmen and ostlers contending one against the other.' Matters proved no better along the route, especially at Ilminster where the peel of bells intended for the introductory *Defiance* service in the down direction rang out for the wrong coach! As an observer put it, 'instead of the new *Defiance* the poor old *Subscription* came trotting nimbly up to the door of the George Inn.'

From time to time an innkeeper would advertise for a partner in setting up a new route. The most common arrangement involved a partner at each end and supplying the horses for the first section or two of the route. Those for the other sections

BULL & MOUTH
WESTERN COACH OFFICE,
40, REGENT CIRCUS, PICCADILLY,

From which place the fastest and best regulated Coaches start to all parts of the Kingdom.

THE NEW ROYAL TELEGRAPH,
To MANCHESTER, in ONE DAY!
THE TELEGRAPH,
To EXETER, in ONE DAY!
THE WONDER,
To SHREWSBURY, in ONE DAY!
THE MAZEPPA,
To HEREFORD, in ONE DAY!
To Brighton and Oxford Ten Times a Day,
&c. &c. &c.
VANS AND WAGGONS TO ALL PARTS DAILY.

		£.	s.	d.
Mr Lea Carriage			6	2
No 12 Porterage				8

THOMAS WEBB,
WILLIAM FELTHAM, } Porters.   £   0 11

Mar 20th   EDWARD SHERMAN & CO.
PROPRIETORS.

N. B. Luggage Carted from any part of the Town.

12,000—Nov. 29, 1836.

This document confirms Mr Lea's booking at the Western Coach Office for a journey on one of Edward Sherman's yellow coaches. Its wording reflects Sherman's reputation for speed. Note that the porters are named and that a number is quoted, probably denoting a form of seat reservation.

would be supplied under arrangements made with inns or posting houses at intermediate points, or from the stables of a landowner or farmer if no suitable inn was available. An advertisement of 1795 regarding the Royal Clarence post coach, which set off at 4am from the Bell & Crown, Holborn and at the same hour from the Half Moon at Exeter, showed the route operators as Thomas Fogg of London, H.Bisgood of Exeter and William Budden of Crewkerne.

The same advertisement carried a promise that parcels and fish would be 'delivered immediately in time for the London markets', a reminder that coach operators derived some useful extra revenue from non-human cargoes, and of the problems once caused to the guard of the Muggleton coach when trying to load Mr Pickwick's oversize cod-fish! With the free luggage allowance only 14lbs and each extra pound costing at least a penny useful sums were derived from the fact that many travellers had to take a fair amount of luggage with them to serve their longer stays and longer journeys.

Coaches were obliged to carry newspapers free and they frequently conveyed other urgent items, either as a matter of policy, as free enterprise on the part of the coachmen or to oblige some friend or acquaintance. There was also some competition between coaches and waggons, especially where one or the other was finding it difficult to get profitable loadings, but on the whole the former only handled the luggage of its passengers and a few urgent, perishable or high-value items.

As many coach services had evolved from a stage waggon service it was not surprising that some firms should operate both. The Whitmarsh family of Taunton, for example, was offering coaches, chariots and hearses 'to every part of the county' in 1729. John Whitmarsh then put on a weekly Exeter to Bath coach in 1740 at a time when he was already running waggons from London to most of the towns in the county from Yeovil to Wiveliscombe and 'at as reasonable Rates as shall be expected.'

Whitmarsh's Taunton - London services feature in the Universal British Directory c1794 and in the 1820s there was a Whitmarsh coach office near the Castle Inn, Taunton at which the *North Devon Telegraph* picked up and dropped its passengers. In 1836 H.Whitmarsh & Co were offering twelve coach seats Taunton to Barnstaple and back Mondays to Saturdays and another nine each way between Taunton and Sidmouth.

Not all the new coach businesses prospered and newspaper notices appeared from time to time recording the cessation of a coach operation. On the other hand some enterprises grew very large indeed, especially at the London end. One of these was that of William James Chaplin who, in 1836, operated the mail route to Falmouth via Ilminster, that via Bath and Wells to Devonport and via Bristol and the New Passage Ferry to Pembroke, as well as other services to Bristol and Exeter. At one period Chaplin had a total of 68 routes, including 14 of the 27 mail contracts, making him the biggest of London's 'big three' operators, with a large complement of vehicles, horses and men. His coaches operated from the Swan with Two Necks in Lad Lane and other strategic loading, booking and picking up points in the area. With the Post Office yard just across the way the evening departure peak for Chaplin's coaches was such a colourful spectacle that crowds of watchers could always be guaranteed.

The Royal Mail

Once it had finally absorbed Palmer's ideas the Post Office steadily built up the number of mail coach routes until it was the biggest concern in the coaching business with over 200 hundred vehicles running in 1811. It acted as the principal by offering contracts to reliable operators who had to provide an approved coach plus horses and driver to run to a laid down schedule on each route. The first standard vehicles were based on John Besant's patent mail coach which was tried out successfully in 1787 and was then manufactured for leasing by the successful route operators. His partner and successor, John Vidler, produced an improved version around 1803, its integrated body allowing the addition of outside passengers, the number authorised rising first to one, then to three, and finally to seven. Since the income from fares went to the operators this change proved a welcome one for them.

To serve the needs of the postal system mail coaches travelled mainly at night, often in convoy over common parts of the route or when there was fog. The morning arrivals in London went to Vidler's premises in Millbank to be serviced prior to their evening departure. Vidlers also trained the guards in emergency repairs and maintenance and a tool kit was carried for this purpose. The guards themselves were Post Office employees and, unlike the drivers, always travelled through to destination. Often ex-Army NCOs, they had to provide written and financial sureties and take a service oath before selection but then had a prestigious and secure position earning 10/6d a week and enjoying a scarlet coat with leather trimmings as one of their perks. The guard was in complete charge of the coach with an over-riding duty to supervise the exchange and safe delivery of the mail. He had a horn to demand the entitlement of his vehicle to absolute road priority and ensure free and speedy passage through the toll gates, also a brace of pistols and a short blunderbuss to reinforce the security of the locked mail box on which he sat.

Short run mail routes might operate with two-horse coaches but those to the West required four. The guards were provided with a numbered chronometer housed in a sealed case and were expected to adhere to a strict journey schedule laid down in a time bill. Actual times for each stage had to be entered against the scheduled times along with the number of passengers carried and any significant incidents.

Many of the Royal Mail guards were recruited from ex-Army personnel. They exchanged their military scarlet coat for the scarlet coat of the Post Office and their Brown Bess musket for the pistol and blunderbuss. Their presence dramatically reduced coach hold-ups and robberies.

All time bills were subsequently scrutinised and inspectors were employed to make spot checks along the route. Time was also important in the years before railway time as the communities along the mail coach routes set their clocks by the guard's chronometer.

Mail coaches changed horses frequently, normally every 7-14 miles, and this was often achieved in less than the five minutes allowed. To maintain their overall speeds of up to 10mph other stops were few and mail to and from the smaller locations was thrown off in a bag or picked up by means of a forked stick. A longer stop might be made in major towns and while the guard sorted the mail the sleepy passengers had to grab whatever sustenance was available and be ready to rejoin their vehicle without delay. Luggage would have to be loaded and unloaded together with the parcels which the operator had taken to improve the notoriously meagre earnings from his operations.

Some stops were dictated entirely by mail transfer requirements. The Old Down Inn was one of these and enjoyed calls by the Bath-Exeter mail coach so that mail could be forwarded on to places like Shepton Mallet, Castle Cary and Bruton. At one period mail coming up from Falmouth and other points in the West of England was unloaded at Old Down and then transferred to the Shepton Mallet to Bristol mail cart for onward movement to Ireland, Midlands and Northern destinations. By 1836 the London to Devonport service was running via Old Down, arriving there at 8.50am on the down journey and at 5.35pm on the up.

The Coaches and Coachbuilders

Apart from the mail coaches there was really no such thing as a standard design for public passenger coaches. The process of evolution did take the coach from its origins as a copy of the first cumbersome private coaches to being a good-looking, functional vehicle capable of carrying a good passenger payload in some degree of safety and comfort, but each route tended to have its own requirements and each local coachbuilder his own favourite forms, materials and construction methods. Important milestones in coach design included the replacement of the early curved roofs by flat ones which would take a load of passengers or their luggage, the introduction of smaller front wheels to aid turning and welcome improvements in brakes and springing. The use of integrated bodies which replaced the rear slung basket with a boot was followed around 1804 by the advent of Obadiah Elliot's elliptical springs which permitted a lower centre of gravity and better horse control from an elevated driving position.

Coaching records, once they had abandoned the expression 'machine' refer, somewhat loosely, to the mail coach, the light coach, to fly and long coaches, to heavy ones, subscription ones, to caravans and to balloon coaches. Balloon and fly tended to be references to speed rather than design and often meant a light coach with just two horses and travelling fast enough to outrun the competition. A major distinction was between the traditional transverse seating and the longitudinal omnibus seating which came increasingly into use for short and medium distances and for feeder services. Some light on the types of coach in use is cast by the 31 medium distance services operating out of Bristol in 1836. Of these, 22 involved coaches carrying four passengers inside and eight outside with the remainder using 4-5, 4-11, 6-0 and 4-4 combinations. The outside load of eleven involved one on the box with the coachman, two on the 'dickey' with the guard and four facing in each direction between them.

Coach construction was usually undertaken at one location but could involve body makers, wheelwrights, coach trimmers, carpenters, specialist blacksmiths, painters and so forth. Almost any type of commonly available wood might be used for the main bodywork, along with iron for axles, underframes, springs and strengthen-

ing. Leather, hides, horsehair, paint, glass and textiles all made a contribution. Bristol in 1837 not only had twenty coach makers but also three coach lamp makers, a coach currier, a spring maker and a coach brass founder. There were also carvers and gilders who specialised in coach work and thirteen coach proprietors operating the finished products, two of them using hearses.

Inside coach passengers enjoyed a reasonable degree of comfort with a wide door leading to an upholstered interior, albeit with straight seat backs guaranteed to test the most supple spine. They also had windows to keep out the elements but those condemned by cost to the exposed areas above the central body had to climb to a height of up to 12ft by using an iron ladder or via the wheel hub, rim and steps in the body panelling. They were then perched on narrow seats, sparsely cushioned with fabric-covered horsehair and provided with a frugally upholstered backrest and perhaps just an iron frame to side and rear. The coach exterior would be more impressive with a bright livery plus route and statutory information and other embellishments. Chaplin's coaches, for example, were red and gold and Sherman's a strong and unmistakable yellow.

The Horses

The most complex aspect of the coaching business was the horse power, the animals themselves together with their feeding, grooming, accommodation, health, equipment and handlers. Horses had long been used for riding and for the chase and these provided the nucleus for breeding as travel increased and the use of the post expanded. Postmaster innkeepers offered horses for hire as well as providing the mounts for post boys, and as early as 1600 a coach and two horses could be

hired in London for ten shillings a day. This was a long way from the thousands of animals that would eventually be required for pulling coaches, chaises and other passenger vehicles but horse breeders, including those in Somerset, responded to the challenge and eventually a good horse would cost anything up to £35.

Initially mail coach horses were limited to a trot and created a demand for fast trotting horses which could work in pairs. With runs averaging about ten miles the horses got to know their portion of the route and the routines of rest and harnessing. They worked in partnership with their ostlers and coachmen and contributed with their instincts to choosing a safe path and dealing with darkness or bad weather on their journeys. Combinations of two, three or six horses were used but the standard stage coach team consisted of four, two 'wheelers' nearest the coach and two 'leaders' at the front. The former, particularly, had to be matched for stride and be sure-footed, especially as they carried the main burden of restraining a coach until brakes became universal. The wheelers affected the balance more than the pair in front and were not interchangeable with them.

Linking coaches and horses involved a complicated but functional system of shafts, chains, reins and harness. Each horse had a bridle and blinkers with the coachman's reins passing via the collar and girth strap. The pull was exerted through the former via straps linking the wheelers with the coach splinter bar and the leaders to a group of bars and swivels located at the end of the central main shaft. The restraining motion was achieved by chains back to the collars of the wheelers, plus a friction brake on the rear wheel rim and a drag shoe placed in front of the rear wheels on severe inclines.

The best operators replaced a third of their horses annually, especially where tight schedules had to be maintained, and might have to provide up to one horse for every mile of road. Others were not so fussy and the state of a coaching business was often apparent in the appearance and condition of its horses. Older animals could be used on the easier route sections and quite a few blind horses were employed but rarely as leaders or among the pairs attached for a steep hill climb. Fortunately few were like the horse of Mr Pickwick's cab driver Sam whose 'weakness' was that if taken out of the shafts it fell down!

The People

Critical to the whole coaching activity were the drivers and guards. Handling a team of up to six horses in all sort of weathers and road conditions and in the confined spaces of towns and inns called for quite exceptional skills. Clad in long coats and tall hats, they were hardy men, not always thoughtful except for the tips that made a large contribution to their earnings, but the underlying picture is one of a high degree of professionalism emerging as the coaching activity itself grew and as the Royal Mail standards became the norm.

Drinking by coachmen seems to have been fairly commonplace in the earlier years and drunkenness was frequently the cause of accidents or injuries. Even so this should not be taken out of perspective for it seemed quite natural for the Rev. Woodforde to buy his post chaise driver a 'dram' at both Old Down and Cannard's Grave on a wintry journey from Bath to Ansford. There were coaching rogues, too, especially when it came to carrying an undeclared passenger or parcel, but there were also heroes and many who just did their job well and cheerfully.

In the 19th century coach driving skills became something of a fashion among the young bucks who would sit beside the regular drivers and be generous if allowed to take the reins from them. Some spirited running was often the result. George Borrow refers to this craze in *The Romany Rye* and comments that it gave some 'low fellows' too high an opinion of themselves and overhigh gratuity expectations. The guards, whose work tended to diminish with faster runs and fewer stops, often found time to develop their musical talents and become proficient on the key bugle. Tom Goodman on the *Subscription* coach is recorded as treating Ilminster folk to Auld Lang Syne and a selection of hymns on one occasion.

Thousands of other people were also linked to the coaching business from those making a direct contribution to the vendors who congregated outside busy inns at coach times. Bridgwater's coach services in 1830, for example, helped to support in the town two coachbuilders (Henry Hawkins and Charles Sutton), two vets, six blacksmiths, three wheelwrights, seven corn factors, six harness makers and over forty taverns and inns. Inns employed waiters, cooks, chambermaids, scullions, ostlers and sometimes people like bootblacks and hairdressers. Some would live in, some attend only when the coaches called and others, like the post boys and postillions, provided their services on a self-employment basis. Porters were another important part of coaching travel and in London used their own printed luggage receipts.

Coaching Inns and Posting Houses

Some town posting houses operated separately, just providing mounts and carriages for local and social travel. Both inns and taverns catered for the refreshment needs of coach travellers, the former obliged to provide sleeping accommodation, the latter barred from doing so. More modest 'hedge inns' were available on many stage waggon routes and provided bed and supper for 1/- a night or less.

Inns varied considerably in size, ranging from the Crown in South Petherton to the plush and expensive White Hart in Bath. The smaller inns might have just a couple of post chaises and six or eight horses but others would be much more extensive. When the Lamb Inn at Bridgwater was put up for sale in March 1820 it was shown as having 'open stables for 100 horses.' In other cases the problems of providing extensive stables were solved by having extra horses 'on call' in other local establishments.

Some of the London coaching inns were huge, especially Chaplin's Swan with Two Necks, Sherman's Bull & Mouth and others like the Bell & Crown. Sherman kept his horses in underground stables but quite often the larger inns would have ground floor stables with bedrooms leading off open galleries above, all surrounding a courtyard where the loading and unloading and other journey preparations took place. Some of the oldest coaching inns in Somerset originated as religious houses - the George & Pilgrim at Glastonbury, the George at Norton

The Bear Inn at Wincanton was a regular calling point for coaches on the Exeter to London route. To London there was one evening service and two in the morning while in the other direction, the Subscription and the Telegraph coaches both called at the same time, making the Bear a rather busy place.

St.Philip and the Luttrell Arms at Dunster are examples - but others consisted of a simple accommodation block with a carriageway entrance to a rear courtyard and stables. Many examples survive.

A good coaching inn would provide parlours, dining rooms and bedchambers for its guests. There would be cellars for the wine, a brewhouse and then the lockups, coachhouses and stables adjacent to the main building. As well as taking coach bookings, the inn might also serve as a venue for courts, balls, auctions, and other community activities and in some places the landlord might trade in commodities like coal, salt or bricks. At coach times the scene at a sizeable inn would become frenetic with travellers milling around, porters attending to the luggage, coachmen seeking a quick 'nip' and post boys straightening their beaver hats and brushing down their short red or blue jackets in order to impress potential chaise or landau hirers.

Costs and Charges

Although William Chaplin made a fortune from the coaching business and Taunton's Whitmarshes survived in it for a century it is doubtful whether the profits were very high in the majority of cases. Coaches cost from £120 to £150 to build which meant a cost of around 3d a double mile to the operating hirer. In 1776 James Woodforde did buy two horses for £27 . 17 . 6d but as demand grew a single coaching horse could cost as much as this, or more. Although they worked only three days out of four and in short shifts, the job of pulling a heavy coach was wearing and horses would need replacing every 3-4 years. There were also feeding, care and stabling costs to be met plus the coachmen's wages.

Then as now, any activity earning money attracted the attention of Government fund raisers. The coaching business was no exception and incurred first a coach 'wheel' tax, then a mileage duty which crept up from a halfpenny to threepence a mile and also a licence fee based on the passenger capacity of the vehicle. Turnpike payments would add about £3 for a hundred miles of route and there were many other incidental expenses like wages for the booking clerks, whale oil for lamps, advertising payments and so on.

Like any transport business a good load factor was critical to profitability. Earnings of around 3d a mile from inside passengers and half that from those outside provided a good return if the coach was full. Fares on fast and mail coaches were higher but they usually had fewer seats. Passengers' luggage also brought in a useful income. For his journey from London to Bath in 1786 James Woodforde paid 30/- for one of the four inside seats plus another 13/- for his excess luggage. Earlier in the same year 12 stones of luggage had cost him 15/-. Hiring a post chaise cost around 1/6d a mile plus another 3d for the post boy's tip and 6d to the ostler at each changeover. Fortunately there were often cut rates on offer like that advertised by W. Hall of the Red Lion, Crewkerne in the Western Flying Post issue of 29 August 1796. Thanking his customers for past favours he also informed them of a 'reduced price of posting to 1/- a mile' and reminded them that he offered 'good accomodation, neat post chaises, good horses and careful drivers.'

On the Road

It is clear from the letters, diaries and other records of those who travelled by public coach that the experience was rarely entirely pleasant, especially in the early years. A short journey over a good road, in one of the better coaches and in decent weather might just be bearable for those who had an inside seat, but even then the journey could be ruined by the company. Coleridge, for example, complained of the peculiarities of his fellow passengers on a Bristol to London journey and of the fact that the greatcoats they were wearing deprived him of enough space to get comfortable. When he travelled on the night mail in the other direction in 1807 he could manage no more than uneasy, fitful dozing and, as a result, felt 'coach-fevered, coach-crazed and coach-stunned.'

Fares for inside seats were appreciably more than those for outside places, often double. From Barnstaple to Taunton the figures were 21/- and 12/- respectively and from Crewkerne to London 28/- and 18/-. For those who could not afford the extra cost of an inside place, and these included women and children, there was no choice but to clamber up the narrow iron ladder to the top of the coach. Clad in the unwieldly dress of the period and holding on to a young child would have made this a daunting experience for any mother. A child on its mother's lap would pay only half fare but would not get any free luggage allowance. In a sad case at St. Albans in 1820 a woman was so engrossed in ensuring the safety of the niece on her lap that she failed to heed the coachman's warning about a low arch and received a blow on the head that broke her spine.

Improvements in coach springing and in road surfaces slowly improved the lot of the coach passenger in terms of both journey times and comfort. Before the expansion period for turnpike trusts and the road construction improvements brought by people like Metcalfe, Telford and Macadam, the most common approach to road building and maintenance was founded on using a base of large stones from a local quarry and filling the surface gaps with smaller stones or field pebbles. Crushing these level was left to passing waggons and coaches and those with broad wheels received financial benefits to encourage this. John Loudon Macadam (1756 to 1836) had a more sophisticated approach and thanks to his strong connections with the West, many a local traveller enjoyed a better journey as a result of Macadam's attention to surfaces as well as to foundations.

Prior to the Macadam benefits every outside traveller was subjected to the constant discomforts of mud, dust, potholes and flying stones. At best he would reach his destination tired, dirty and unnerved by having to cling to his neighbour or to the tiny protective ironwork at the end of the seat. At worst a wheel might collapse or come off and the coach be overturned, or it might come to grief disputing the narrow roadway with a lumbering waggon. Racing and competitive running by rival services were by no means unknown nor without their casualties.

Charging a snow drift

Understandably, bad weather greatly affected coach travel. Indeed, in the early years many coach services operated only in the summer. In January 1820, after a hard frost, the thaw which followed resulted in the fracture of one of the iron ribs of Hill's Bridge in Totterdown, Bristol. The morning coaches from London and Bath had to be diverted to Bedminster Bridge where work on the approach road was still taking place. The condition of the road and a dispute over the right of passage with a heavy waggon resulted in one coach tipping over and sending the coachman and two outside passengers hurtling down the river bank. They were only saved from the swollen stream by clinging to a sack of oats which had been thrown off with them and which they managed to hang on to until bystanders came to the rescue.

In this Bedminster Bridge incident there were plenty of willing hands to right the coach which duly completed its journey, a reminder of just how deeply travellers were involved in the fortunes of their vehicle. If its load was too much for the horse team to manage on a hill and it was not one where extra animals were normally attached the able-bodied passengers were expected to get out and walk. If the coach got stuck in mud or slipped off the road everyone had to contribute to the lifting and pushing needed to get the journey restarted. In really bad weather coachmen would not set out unless they believed they could get through, but some breakdowns could be neither anticipated nor avoided and the unhappy coach occupants would face a long wait while help was obtained from the nearest inn. Mail coach guards had to give priority to their letters and, in the case of a mishap, would take one of the horses and make sure that the mail got through, with helping the stranded passengers a definite second priority.

Coleridge records enduring a 3-hour storm while travelling by coach from London to Nether Stowey via Bath and Keats, on a journey to Southampton in 1817, got so cold that he changed his outside seat for one inside. Others did not fare so well for five years earlier the temperature dropped so low that when a Bath-bound coach arrived at Chippenham it was found that two passengers had frozen to death and another was dying. Something similar happened on a London to Exeter coach in 1820. After encountering exceptional cold and snow in Somerset the coachman realised that a woman on the top with him seemed completely numb. With the help of fellow passengers he got her into the warmth of the next inn but she died within half an hour. Straw, foot warmers, heavy clothing, blankets and sacks were essentials on a coach journey in periods of severe cold, and the occasional nip from a flask might also prove a wise and welcome restorative.

To anyone undertaking a long journey good coaching inns were a great blessing. At stops made only to change horses there might only be enough time for passengers to alight or clamber aboard in the short period while the ostler and his helper removed the cloths from the fresh horses, unhooked the traces of the tired ones and backed their replacements into place. Longer daytime stops might be anything from ten to forty minutes depending on the schedule, how well it was being maintained and any connections to be made. The passengers would mostly have time to alight, refresh themselves with tea, coffee or wine - sometimes served in the 'travellers' room' - and then rejoin the coach after any visit to the fairly elementary toilet facilities.

Where an overnight stay was involved, arrival at a decent hour could easily mean an excellent supper with a choice of cold meats, pies, steak, ham, kidneys, poached eggs, buttered toast, muffins and wine, beer or hot, strong tea. But not all inns stayed open for late or unexpected travellers and pressures on the accommodation available might mean a night in a pokey attic, sharing a bed or having a bed made up by the parlour fire. Many forward departures were made quite early the following morning when sleepy travellers would be roused by the boots or porter, who would expect a tip for the service, and then would have just about enough time to bolt down coffee and biscuits before parting with more cash for the accommodation, the waiter and the chambermaid. Finally the porter would call out the name and destination of the departing coach and expect a further reward for loading the luggage. Once on the road the traveller would have leisure to discover whether the bed bugs had been active at this particular inn.

Without doubt the character of the coach driver and guard would make a lot of difference to the wellbeing and enjoyment of their passengers. Many were cheerful, independent and skilled people with a high regard for their animals and for the people and goods in their care. Like most transport men they did a sound, professional job with competence, imagination and humour. Occasionally things got a little out of hand as happened with John Hex and the *Tally Ho* coach on the last stage of a journey to Exeter. A report at the time records:-

'Recently, when the 'Tally Ho' coach pulled up at the inn of the last stage for changing horses before reaching Exeter, a heavy rainstorm commenced. Immediately after starting, in order to shelter from the rain, John Hex, the coachman, crept into the front boot of the coach, and in this position drove the horses through Venn and Applington, causing quite a consternation amongst the inhabitants, who thought the horses had run away without a coachman.

Tommy Waters, the guard, fancying something was unusual, peeped over the top of the luggage on the roof, and seeing the horses going faster than common, and no driver, quietly got off behind and in doing so broke his leg.

Just before entering the city Hex stealthily emerged from his concealment, took his seat on the box and drove up to the New London Inn in his usual style.

Shortly after a lot of people came driving and riding up to learn the fate of the coach and horses, which they vowed had no driver as it passed through several villages; while Hex for his part stoutly asserted that he never left the coach, and had driven all the way without a passenger except for the two inside, who were unaware of the act of the sportive coachman.'

What poor Tommy Waters thought of this is not recorded!

Over the years coach drivers brought the handling of their heavy vehicle and its team of spirited horses to a fine art. Guards, too, honed their skills and many became something of a virtuoso on the horn and its successor, the key bugle. Popular tunes were often played in addition to the calls to herald approaching or leaving an inn. Mail coach guards would sound a clear warning of their approach to a tollgate as a reminder that they, along with churchgoers, local farmers and the military, were entitled to free passage. Regular stage coaches usually paid their tolls on a weekly basis but those making a journey by post chaise had to pay their own tolls for each journey.

Coachmen would normally salute one another on the road and give assistance where it was needed. As the top men of their profession they were often impatient of slow waggons and anything else that hindered their progress. Drovers with their animals and the 5-horse coal carts of the North Somerset coalfield were less of a problem for they dodged the tollgates wherever they could. As the number of newspapers increased, coaches played a major role in their distribution but coachmen were also great purveyors of headline news and of more informal snippets. Coaches might even sport a few strings of bunting to celebrate a victory in an elec-

Turnpike tollhouses varied immensely in design but were rarely as elaborate as this one near Chard. They were always located so as to capture as much business as possible and, frequently, as in this case, stood in the angle of a road junction. Toll rights were auctioned annually.

tion or one of the many foreign conflicts of the period.

In the early coaching years travellers were at some risk of being robbed. Nearer London there were a few highwaymen of the Dick Turpin variety but in the West Country the greatest danger was from footpads and those made desperate by lack of work or other deprivation. Post boys were especially vulnerable, and sometimes venal, but the introduction of mail coaches, too fast to catch easily and provided with an armed guard, rapidly reduced the risks of travel. The sight of a bell-mouthed blunderbuss, loaded with a dozen pea-sized pieces of shot and sometimes fitted with a bayonet, became a powerful deterrent. Additionally the growth in banking steadily reduced the money and valuables travellers needed to take with them.

By the 19th century coach travel was not too uncomfortable for people of means who could not only afford the inside fare plus all the journey extras, but could also pick a service that avoided most of the travel hardships. In addition to the journey fare there would be a further 3/6d to pay for an overnight stay at a decent inn, plus 2/- for dinner and 1/- for breakfast. Tips for the porter, waiter, chambermaid and coachmen would cost as much again bringing the total cost for a journey, with luggage and over a medium distance, to approaching £2.10s. Although beyond ordinary people, this represented reasonable value when compared with twice as much for using a post chaise, the £200 annual cost of running your own vehicle, four saddle-sore days on horseback or roughing it on a stage waggon because of a slender purse.

The Coaching Heyday

In the first twenty years of the 19th century public coach services in the most populous parts of Britain roughly doubled in number. Within this rise there was some change of relative importance between alternative routes and a variety of new routes were added. The upshot was that nearly all towns of any significance had at least one coach service a day while over a hundred a week linked major cities like Bristol and Bath. The increase was to continue well into the 1830s before railways began to make the first inroads into the West Country traffic.

Fuelling this growth was the end of the Napoleonic wars and the resultant Second Peace of Paris. After faltering for a while economic and industrial growth resumed and affected most communities. Weston-super-Mare, for example, added a second hotel in 1819 to the 1810 Royal and began to be served by coaches conveying the adventurous early visitors. In an advertisement of 1816 T.Clark & Co 'begged leave to inform the public' - such was the language convention of the period - that a four-horse coach with room for four inside would begin running from the Talbot Inn at Bath and the Coach Office at Temple Gate, Bristol to Uphill and Weston-super-Mare. Leaving at 9am and returning the following day the route was via Backwell, Congresbury, Banwell and Hutton. There was also to be a caravan three times a week for carrying luggage. In 1828 the *Aurora* began another Bristol - Weston service, leaving the Plume of Feathers in Wine Street at 8.45am, changing horses at Cleeve and reaching its destination at 11.45am.

Within the overall pattern of more and better services a few of the old problems lingered on. Drink was still one of them and a drunken coachman who fell from his box near Alveston in 1806 paid a high price for his intoxication when the coach wheels passed over him and caused his death. Fortunately the guard was made of different stuff and was able to bring the runaway horses under control and save his passengers from probable disaster. Gangs of ne'er-do-wells were still terrorising routes around the Kingswood Forest area of Bristol as late as 1814 but this had more to do with the pay and conditions applying in 19th century coal mines than with the coaching trade itself. Also in 1814 a Chew Magna man, William Fowler was shot and killed on Dundry Hill by a highwayman. This reflected the trend to rob lone travellers rather than risk confrontation with the now more protected coaches. William Fowler's headstone can be seen in St. Andrew's churchyard in Chew Magna and the inscription describing the unfortunate event is still legible.

The 1820s saw some transfer of traffic from mail to stage coaches. With travel safety more assured the higher fares and night time journeys of the mail contractors could not compete with a good, fast daytime schedule. Even so the traditional mail routes were maintained and places like Gloucester sent a daily coach to Bath plus the *Wellington* and the *Phoenix* to Bristol. There was a regular 9am service from Cheltenham to Bath provided by the *Original Post Coach* running via Gloucester and Rodborough and a 2pm departure when the *York House Coach* performed the journey via Painswick and Stroud.

On the sidelines of the early 19th century changes was the attempt to apply steam propulsion to the coaching business. This had its origins in 1801 when, on Christmas Eve, Richard Trevithick's novel steam carriage successfully climbed the

1 in 20 of Beacon Hill at Camborne. An improved version, fitted with a stage-coach body, ran in London soon after. Other designs made desultory appearances in the years that followed, with a heavy steam carriage by Goldsworthy Gurney making a successful return trip from London to Bath in 1829. Like an elongated stagecoach in appearance, Gurney's vehicle provoked some lively antagonism from those whose livelihood depended on horses. The worst incidents were at Melksham, a town hugely dependent on its coaching traffic. Stones were thrown and two passengers injured, the steamer then having to take refuge in a local brewery yard watched over by the parish constables. Wisely the return working was timed to pass through Melksham at night! A different Gurney design subsequently ran between Gloucester and Cheltenham but the steam coach never really surmounted its technical problems.

Between London and Bath there were two main coaching routes, both leaving the capital via Hounslow and the six miles of 'galloping ground' which followed and then diverging after Marlborough to pass either via Calne and Chippenham or via Devizes and Melksham. In 1830 each was used by about fifty coaches a week. As well as the ones that ran through to Bristol there were two services terminating at Bath, the *White Hart* via Devizes and the *York House* via Chippenham. The *Star* ran between Reading and Bristol via Devizes while the *Exeter Mail* travelled the same way to Bath before turning south towards Wells.

On the Exeter road the *Age* and the *Auxiliary Mail* still used the senior route via Dorchester. The *Defiance* and *Subscription* coaches took the 19th century equivalent of the A303 through Wincanton, Ilchester and Ilminster, while the *Traveller* and the *Quicksilver Mail* used the A30 route through Yeovil and Chard. The *North Devon Telegraph* also ran east-west, passing through Wincanton to Langport and then on to Barnstaple via Taunton. It took twenty hours on this first part of the journey before H.Whitmarsh and Co took over for the remaining stretch into Devon.

A microcosm of Somerset coaching services in 1830 was provided by Bridgwater which originated three long distances coaches and was a calling point for eight others. The former were made up of the 10.30am daily service by the *Hero* from the Globe Inn to London via Wells and Frome, the *Duke of Wellington* from the Bristol Arms to Bristol itself at 10am on Mondays, Wednesdays and Fridays, and the *Industry* which left the London Inn for Minehead on the same days. The latter carried forward any passengers from the Bristol direction brought in on the 2pm arrival of the *Comet*.

On weekdays the through services were made up of:-

> *Royal Mail,* Exeter-London via Bath and calling at the Crown Inn at 12.50pm in each direction,
> *Royal Mail,* Bristol-Barnstaple, Clarence Hotel, 1.10pm down, 1.50pm up,
> *Royal Devon,* Exeter-London via Bristol, Globe at midnight down, George 9.15pm up,
> *Old Bath Coach,* Exeter-Bath, Clarence down at noon, George 12.30pm up,
> *Times,* Birmingham-Falmouth, 12.15pm from the Clarence down, noon up,

with the Bristol-Barnstaple *Freemason,* the Taunton-Bath *Union* and the Bristol-Exeter *Comet* providing extra capacity on alternate days.

This pattern gave Bridgwater people a choice of three services to London, five to Exeter, three towards North Devon, four to Bath and six to Bristol including the extensions to Birmingham and Falmouth provided by the *Times.* In addition three ships conveyed London passengers, one also named *Hero* like its coach counterpart, four sailed to Bristol and two each to Cardiff, Swansea, Gloucester and

Bath was well served by both mail and stage coaches despite High Street Street delightfully uncrowded in this 1827 representation.

Liverpool. Of the six inns dealing with coaches only one, the Bristol Arms, was also involved in the waggon business. Some coaches called at the George one day and the Globe the next while the *Freemason* called at both.

By the 1830s coach speeds had reached their ceiling. There was a service from London to Birmingham that averaged 12mph and one to Manchester at an overall 10mph, but the figure on West Country routes rarely bettered just over 9mph despite the fast stretches west of Hounslow and Hartford Bridge. Among the best were the achievements of *Cooper's Day Coach* which covered the 122 miles from London to Bristol via Calne in 13 hours and the 18 hours taken by the *Telegraph* to get to Exeter, both averaging 9.3mph. This figure was nearly matched by the *Quicksilver Mail* on the London to Devonport section with the whole journey to Falmouth, including horse changes and the Saltash Ferry crossing, being completed in just under 30 hours. This Chaplin service was touching 20mph on some sections and the rival Sherman service took only three hours more for its longer route via Dorchester and Okehampton.

In 1836 the 8pm mail departures from the GPO Yard in London included coaches for Exeter via Crewkerne, for Falmouth via Ilminster, Devonport via Bath and Wells, and for Pembroke via Bristol. Bristol also had cross country mail routes to Portsmouth, Bath, Bideford, Liverpool and Manchester. For mail arriving at Taunton at 12.35pm off the Devonport coach there were connecting services on at 2pm for Sidmouth and 2.15pm for Minehead. Mail speeds were comparable with those of the best stage coaches, 9.3mph to Exeter and nearly 10mph to Bristol.

In addition to these mail coach services, the major towns of the region were also busy with stage coach business. The General Stage Coach Company's office at the Rummer Hotel in Bristol, for example, handled a day coach and a night coach on the London route although these were slower than those the Cooper's Company dealt with at their office at 6 High Street. The *Regulator* ran from the White Lion in Broad Street with a choice of 7am or 4pm departures and the *Emerald* followed at 7.45am but took the Devizes route. The 5.15pm *Monarch* started from the White Hart and then called at the White Lion before heading on via Bath and Chippenham. In the down direction there were five early departures from London for Bristol and four in the afternoon. Five coaches linked London and Exeter through Somerset, two in the morning and three in the afternoon.

At this period the non-London services were also extensive. There were single-coach routes from Bath to Bathford, Bradford-on-Avon, Cheltenham, Lyme Regis, Poole, Reading, Shrewsbury, Sidmouth, Taunton, Trowbridge, Warminster and

Westbury. Then there were two services to Chippenham, Southampton and Weymouth, three to Exeter and no less than five to fashionable Clifton. Four Birmingham coaches arrived in Bath each day and three came from Oxford. Bristol originated services to some sixty places including the ferry across the Severn at Old Passage and the Stroudwater junction between the canal route from the Thames and the river. With no such aids as modern destination indicators or timetable websites there must have been many periods of noise and confusion as coaches vied for passage and passengers, people voiced queries and anxieties, innkeepers solicited custom, and coachmen gave directions, all while tips were being offered and solicited, luggage and parcels loaded and unloaded and the handling of restive and eager horses demanded its own special skills from the harassed ostlers.

Ten of the coach routes from Bristol were to satellite locations within a fifteen-mile radius. They ran on days and at times influenced by markets and other local needs and were largely the province of single operators. Of the ten, only the Thornbury coach carried outside passengers, and then only two. The others had four or six inside seats and probably had more in common with a post chaise than with a full blown coach. An exception was the service provided to Kingswood Hill by H.Budgett & Co which had room for nine inside, probably on three transverse seats. Of some 36 Bristol coach operators no less than 30 had only a single route. The main large concerns were:-

> William Clift of The Feathers in Wine Street,
> T.Hawkins of Temple Gate,
> John Townsend & Son of Corn Street,
> John Bland of 60 Broadmead,
> J.Niblett & Co of the White Lion, Broad Street

Between them they provided most of the longer distance coach services like those to Brighton, Cheltenham, Hereford, Minehead and Weymouth. For these routes coaches with 4-8 seating were the norm although Clift had a 4-11 coach on the Exeter service. For the medium distance destinations like Frome, Calne and Weston-super-Mare both 4-5 and 4-8 configurations were in use.

J.Niblett & Co was the biggest of the Bristol coach businesses. Their operations ranged from the *Monarch* service to London through the important routes to Brighton, Cheltenham, Exeter, Hereford, Taunton and Weymouth to three very local services. Each of the Niblett routes had at least one coach operating Mondays to Saturdays so that the company would have needed around thirty coaches to ful-

44

fil its commitments.

Public coaching activity reached its zenith around 1840. At Bridgwater, for example, the number of services had almost doubled since 1830. Most of the coach
names had changed, too, and were now an imaginative and extrovert mixture
embracing *Exquisite* and *Economist, Alcesta* and *Estafette* and *Westonian* and
John O'Groat. From the marketing point of view *Swiftsure* was an excellent name
choice and its operation lived up to the implication. Leaving the Royal Clarence
every Monday, Wednesday and Friday at 7.30am *Swiftsure* reached the Bell &
Crown in Holborn at 9pm having travelled by way of Ashcott, Street, Glastonbury,
Wells, Shepton Mallet, Frome, Warminster, Amesbury and Andover. A fresh driver took over at the latter point leaving the Bridgwater coachman-proprietor to wait
there for the next day's down service which left Holborn at 7.30am. This was a
high pressure operation for the coaches would need to be serviced overnight at
each end, the horses groomed and cared for, ticketing, taxes and money matters
looked after, all leading to Mr. Johns the proprietor having very little time for
leisure.

On the Exeter route the *Telegraph* and the *Vivid* had joined the earlier *Defiance,
Subscription, Traveller* and *Quicksilver.* The newcomers used the Ilminster route
to which the *Quicksilver* had now changed so that only the *Traveller* still took the
Chard road. The *Telegraph* was the fastest of the newcomers, completing the up
journey to Hyde Park Corner and Aldgate in eighteen hours including time for
breakfast at Ilminster and dinner at Andover. The down mail to Exeter via Bath
and Old Down was doing even better at this time by covering the 160 miles to
Taunton at an average of 9.6mph.

Among the cross-Somerset services in 1840 were the *Wellington* and the *John Bull*
which linked Bath and Weymouth via Bruton and services like the *Red Rover* and
the *Royal Dorset* between Bristol and Weymouth. There was also a Bristol via
Bath route to Lyme Regis run by the *Retaliator* and one by the *Westonian* from
Bristol to Barnstaple via Weston-super-Mare. An unusual route configuration was
that of the *Magnet* which ran from London to Taunton via Southampton and
Yeovil.

Today Pipers Inn still stands in Ashcott at the junction of the roads from Taunton,
Bridgwater, Somerton and Street, and many a traveller still stops there for refreshment. It was equally busy in 1840 and the staff always had to be up and ready for
the early post chaise hirers and for the 9am call of the *Swiftsure* on its alternate day

journey to London. It would call again at 8pm on the following day on the way back to Bridgwater. But noon to 3pm was the really hectic period at Pipers Inn. The *White Hart* coach to Taunton and Exeter would arrive promptly at mid-day, followed by the down *Mail* at 12.30pm and both *Union* coaches, one to Bath and the other to Taunton, at 12.45pm. The big dining rooms would have been crowded and the staff busy with providing food, arranging chaise hire and the other paraphernalia of attending to the requirements of a very individualistic clientele. There would have been no let up in the pressure until after the up *White Hart* had left at 2pm and the *London Mail* an hour later.

The 'Pipers' at Ashcott was a busy inn open long hours to cater for the coach traffic to and from London and for those who needed to hire post chaises to commence or complete their journeys.

At Wincanton four inns were kept busy with coaching business, the Dolphin, the Greyhound, the Trooper and the Bear. Of these the Bear was the busiest with the *Telegraph, Subscription* and *Defiance* all calling on their journeys between London and Exeter and the alternate-day *Wellington* briefly interrupting its journeys to Bath and Weymouth. Some of the calls were at night so landlord Thomas Grist and his staff rarely slept normal hours. At the Dolphin further up High Street, George Forward was mine host for *Magnet* patrons while in the Market Place the *Mail* used John Bailey's Greyhound Hotel and Posting House and Thomas White's Trooper Inn handled the *North Devon* and *John Bull* coaches.

By the summer months of 1840 the new railway route from London to Bristol had reached its halfway point. Ahead, construction work scarred the countryside and sounded its warning of impending change. Even so coaching activity further west was still on the increase. In Bath, William Lane & Co, operating from the 'Royal Mail Coach and Van Establishment' at the Lion Hotel, had just added two new services to an already impressive list viz the 8.30am *Vampire* to Exeter and the *Phoenix* which left for Poole thirty minutes later. Lane & Co handled Royal Mail services to London, Portsmouth and Southampton, to the West Country and to West Wales while his noon mail coach to Cheltenham offered the inducement of conveying passengers 'at coach (presumably stage coach) fares'. In the Lane departure schedule there was an early example of an 'interval service' which was made up of coaches leaving for Bristol every hour on the hour from 5am to 7pm. The most prestigious service was probably the *New Royal Mail* which carried all those travelling to northern destinations. Quite significantly the destinations listed for this service included:-

Manchester and Liverpool - *New Royal Mail* in 17 hours,
 by Railway from Birmingham, evenings at a quarter to six.

Coming of the Railways

When the Stockton & Darlington Railway opened in 1825 its primary purpose was to improve the facilities for moving coal. The company itself had nothing to do with carrying passengers for its first eight years although it did allow contractors to operate horse-drawn coaches in between the movement of coal trains. Such coaches stopped wherever there was a demand and worked in conjunction with local inns in much the same manner as their road counterparts. The big change came with the opening of the Liverpool & Manchester Railway in 1830 and its carriage of businessmen between those two cities right from day one. This was a milestone in the inland movement of people with few resemblances to the traditional patterns except in terms of vehicle design and travel documentation. Before the decade was out there was a trunk railway route between London and the North

West and the GPO had secured statutory authority to transfer the movement of mail to the expanding network of trains.

These developments signalled the beginning of the end for traditional road coaching over trunk routes. The activity which had employed 30,000 men and 150,000 horses at its peak and offered passenger conveyance over a network of some 4,000 coaches was now to enter a period of dramatic change. Apart from catering for a few traditionalists and those unwilling to trust themselves to the new steam monsters, coaches could not compete with the trains when they did start running.

Maidenhead Station opened 1838

The opening of the first section of the Great Western Railway in 1838 marked the start of a period of immense upheaval for the West Country coaching business.

However it was to be many years before the railway network penetrated every part of the country. This provided a lot of time for adapting and although the loss of a trunk route put many a coach company out of business the overall pattern saw operators taking up a new role that supplemented the trains and gave them access to communities they could not serve directly. William Chaplin was one of the coach magnates who read the writing on the wall early and clearly. His Chaplin & Horne partnership became an agent for the London & Birmingham Railway and provided freight and passenger feeder services to and from its trains. He later invested in the London & South Western Railway and was twice its chairman. In contrast his rival, Sherman, tried to fight the trains and ruined himself in the process.

The Great Western Railway scheme was the first to affect the West Country in this way. The idea of a railway between London and Bristol had been mooted back in the 1820s but it was to be 1838 before the first section of the line, from London to Maidenhead, was opened. The GWR had clearly set its sights on the age-old business carried along the London-Bath road and a contemporary account in The Times recorded:-

'As evidence of the traffic that might be expected on the opening of this portion of the railway, it was stated that the line runs nearly parallel with the Great Western and Uxbridge roads, on which the average number of vehicles passing daily has been ascertained to be as follows:-

	Colnbrook	Hanwell	Total
Stage coaches	77	46	123
Post chaises and private carriages	105	38	143
Phaetons and gigs	95	45	140
Mounted saddle horses	78	27	105
Spring carts	59	47	106
Stage waggons	80	52	132

To the foregoing must be added the ten Taunton, Bridgewater (sic) and Exeter coaches, going by Staines and performing 19 journies daily, also the 27 coaches running to and from Bristol and Bath, performing 54 journies daily, exclusive of the 20 daily journies by the coaches passing through Bath to and from London and Bristol, the passengers from all of which must eventually pass over the railway.'

The general pattern associated with the opening of new railways produced some extra coach passengers during the construction periods as those associated with each new line had to survey and resource materials in connection with the route. Then, as each section of the line was opened, displaced coaches turned to connecting with the trains either to enable the users to complete their journeys to the ultimate destination or to provide a link to off-route towns. As the Great Western advanced towards Bristol between 1838 and 1841 coaches realigned their routes to link Steventon with Oxford, Swindon with Marlborough and Chippenham with Devizes. The effect was a threefold increase in coach movement on the latter route but something like a 90% drop on the old road through Marlborough.

As coach services adjusted to the pattern of railway expansion, some turnpike trusts altered the location of affected gates to gather tolls from the new feeder routes. This was little more than a rearguard action and hardly influenced the gradual deterioration of turnpike finances. By the middle of the century turnpike tolls in Somerset barely covered interest and working expenses and less than 2% of the £320,000 debt burden was being paid off annually.

The pattern of railway expansion in the West developed from the June 1841 completion of the GWR main line from London to Bristol. A couple of weeks earlier trains of the Bristol & Exeter Railway had reached Bridgwater, with extension to Taunton following in 1842 and completion through to Exeter in May 1844. Main railway events of the 1850s were the progressive extension of the route through Frome and Yeovil to Weymouth between 1851 and 1857 and the first mid-Somerset penetrations to Shepton Mallet and to Glastonbury, Wells and on into Dorset. Watchet was reached in 1862 and in the early 1870s the Taunton-Wiveliscombe line was extended to Barnstaple, Bath was joined to Evercreech and the Watchet to Minehead extension was completed. Northwards from Bristol trains had begun running on the Bristol & Gloucester Railway in July 1844 linking at the latter point with those of the Birmingham & Gloucester Railway. Each main line was also adding branches over this period.

From its peak in 1840 the public coaching business began a period of accelerating change. The London-Bristol through route had been decimated by 1842 with only a couple of coaches running on the trunk portion through Marlborough but with some increases on shorter routes centred on Melksham. Bridgwater recorded only one remaining coach service, that provided by the *Prince of Wales* which ran to Minehead every day except Sundays in summer and alternate days in winter. It was based at the Royal Clarence Hotel which had its own link with the B&E railway station by courtesy of Sutton's omnibus. Omnibuses also ran to Langport, Taunton and Stogursey, along with ships to London, Liverpool and Cardiff and a barge service on the Taunton & Bridgwater Canal 'occasionally'.

Suggesting that coach operators made some recovery from the initial shock of railway competition, an extra omnibus was put on from Bridgwater to Yeovil in 1844 and a *White Hart* coach reappeared in the Bridgwater directory. This was routed via Glastonbury and Wells to Bath and, apparently, went forward from there to Gloucester and Cheltenham on the following day. At this time Bath still listed twenty four coach destination areas but the pattern had changed from the early one of services in all directions to a much more discernible one. For example, passengers for the North and North West were all conveyed to Gloucester on the *White Hart* or the *Mercury* and transferred to trains there. There were still plenty of coaches from Bath to South Coast destinations, including one to Brighton with an overnight stop at Southampton. Surprisingly there were also three coaches still running to Exeter, the *Coronet, L'Hirondelle* and *Eclipse,* with the *Nonpareil* passing through there on its way to Plymouth and Devonport. This on-going coaching activity plus the many private and rental coaches still kept eight Bath coach builders and harness makers in business.

Elsewhere in Somerset the *North Devon* still linked London and Barnstaple on alternate days and the *Royal Mail* and the *Defiance* continued to run to Exeter. The county was still bisected by *Red Rover* and the *Royal Dorset* on their way to Weymouth but a new breed of coach was now emerging, sometimes referred to as a 'Railway Coach' because it made connection with a railway station and often a specific train. Examples included a coach from Weymouth to Taunton via Chard and one from Wells to take Exeter passengers to Taunton station. Nor were smaller places excluded from these increasing road/rail links, a good example being the Jarvis omnibus which left Axbridge twice a day to take people to the B&E station at Banwell, later Puxton & Worle. Inns had also sprung up at most railway stations and it may not be too fanciful to think that some former coaching landlords may have moved there.

The dramatic impact of the new GWR railway to Bristol was to result in many coach services being abandoned and to coaches like this one eventually ending up in museums.

By the time the 19th century reached its halfway point railways were dominating the long distance passenger transport business with coaches relegated to cross-country and feeder routes. Ilminster, for example, still had four routes but all were firmly linked with Taunton. The *Royal Dorset Mail* called at the Dolphin at 10.30am on its way from Bridport to Taunton, the *Retaliator Mail* stopped at the George Hotel at 11.15am before going to the same destination 'to meet the Express train', and the Weymouth-Taunton *Prince Albert Coach* followed at 2pm. An 'Accommodation Omnibus' went from the Grapes to Taunton at 8am on three days a week and to Yeovil on Fridays at 8.30am. Another Yeovil to Taunton service was provided by the *Fairy Mail Coach* from 1850 to at least 1861. It was a daily service with morning calls at Martock's White Hart and then the Langport Arms, stopping there again on the mid-afternoon return.

At the beginning of the 20th century steam propulsion re-emerged on the road transport scene and some steam buses were operational for ten years or so until overtaken by the petrol-driven vehicles pioneered in Eastbourne in 1903. For the fifty years from 1850 to 1900 coaches had continued their important but subsidiary role of catering for local movement and acting as railway feeders. Wright's Bristol

Steam Packet & Railway Timetables for September 1853 listed a whole page of the latter. It showed that you could, if you were good at rising early, take a cab from White Ladies' Pike to the station at Temple Gate for 1/8d, catch the 1.25am mail train to Exeter and alight at Tiverton Junction for the 3.25am coach to Barnstaple. The cost would be around 30/-. However, a longer stay in bed and a saving of a few shillings could be achieved by going to Ilfracombe instead and using the 10am train departure and its 12.30pm onward coach connection. Or for the really wealthy there was the option of taking your carriage and horses on the train with you. Doing so from Bristol to Exeter would set you back 40/- for a 4-wheel carriage and another 54/- for two horses to pull it.

The railway finally reached Minehead in 1874 and took away the long distance coach business but coaches were still needed to serve the area to the west. The Wellington Hotel, traditional starting point for many a stage coach journey, adapted well to the a motor car age and continued to thrive.

During this second half of the century the coaching business functioned well and profitably in its new sphere. The glamour days may have passed but there was still a good and useful living to be made by linking stations with hotels, villages with their local town and acting as links between or extensions of the steadily expanding train services. A typical example is provided by the twelve years before the Taunton to Watchet line was extended to Minehead, the latter being served during this period by a daily coach to and from Williton station and a summer-only connection to Lynton. The same area is also notable for the coach service which ran from the Ship Inn at Porlock well into the 20th century until motor vehicles became powerful enough to tackle the 1 in 4 of Porlock Hill.

The final coaching years were the province of cabs, horse omnibuses and every imaginable type of private coach. Horse-drawn vehicles provided the transport for thousands of works and club outings and traditional coaches were still used on a great deal of the expanding excursion business. They may not have galloped the great coaching routes demanding passage with an imperious bugle but Weston-super-Mare, at least, maintained the tradition of colourful coach names. It offered its land and steamer visitors trips to Sand Bay, Cheddar and Burnham in coaches named *Tallyho, Rosebud, Pride of the West* and *Venture.*

The Whip Collector

Acknowledgements and Sources

Although there is a significant amount of literature dealing with the coaching era as a whole, very little seems to have been written about coaching in the area covered by this book. No doubt this is partly due to the fact that the coaching business was not overly concerned with handing down tidy records so that, despite their limitations, much reliance has had to be placed on newspapers, the early directories, personal diaries and other fragmentary sources. Access to these has generously been made available at the Somerset Record Office, by David Bromwich at the Somerset Studies Library, at Bristol, Bath and other area libraries and by Steve Bailey at the Bath Postal Museum. We are particularly grateful for the support of the latter and of the Bristol Industrial Archaeological Society.

Works consulted include:-
David Mountfield's *The Coaching Age* (Hale, 1976) and *Stage and Mail Coaches* (Shire, 2003); *Shepton Mallet - An Historical & Postal Survey,* Eric H.Ford, 1958; *An Illustrated History of Stagecoaches and Carriages,* Ivan Sparkes (Spurbooks, 1975); *Journey by Stages 1660-1840,* Stella Margetson (Cassell, 1967); *Directory of Stage Coach Services 1836, Alan Bates* (David & Charles, 1969); *Turnpike to Iron Road,* Col.H.C.B.Rogers (Seeley, Service, 1961); *Journeys in England,* ed Jack Simmons (David & Charles, 1969); *Coaching Days and Coaching Ways,* W.Outram Tristram (Macmillan, 1893); *The Old Roads of England,* Sir William Addison (Batsford, 1980); *The Story of Passenger Transport in Britain,* J.Joyce (Ian Allan, 1967); *Steam on the Road,* David Burgess White (Hamlyn, 1973); *Road Travel and Transport in Gloucestershire,* Nicholas Herbert (Alan Sutton & Glos County Library, 1985); *Coaching Days in the Midlands,* Brian Haughton (Quercus, 1997); *Stage Coach Operations Through Wiltshire,* John Chandler (S.Wilts. Ind. Arch. Soc, 1980); *Horse Drawn Vehicles Since 1760,* Arthur Ingram (Blandford, 1977); *John Palmer and the Mailcoach Era,* Sally Davis (Bath Postal Museum, 1984); *Paupers and Pig Killers,* ed Jack Ayres (Alan Sutton, 1984); *The Diary of a West Country Physician 1684-1726,* ed Edmund Hobhouse (Simpkin Marshall, 1934); *Letters from Bath,* John Penrose (Alan Sutton, 1983); *The Diary of A Country Parson 1758-1802,* James Woodforde (OUP, 1978); *The Annals of Bristol,* John Latimer (George's/Kingsmead, 1970); *The Posthumous Papers of the Pickwick Club,* Charles Dickens. Also *A New and Correct Plan of the City of Bath c1795* (SRO); *Somerset County Herald, London Gazette, Taunton Courier* and *Western Flying Post;* the account book of Solomon Franklin of Nettlecombe; the *Great Western Railway Magazine (1890);* Wright's *Bristol Steam Packet and Railway Timetables, September 1853; Univseral British Directory c1794;* Slater's *Directory of Somersetshire, 1830;* Mathews *Commercial List 1837; Somerset Gazette Directory, 1840;* Pigot & Co's *Directory of Somersetshire, 1944;* Hunt's *Directory, 1848* and Morris's *Directory of Somerset & Bristol, 1872.* The Bath Postal Museum kindly gave permission for the use of the illustration on the front cover. Photographs and other illustrations are from the authors' collection supplemented by engravings from *Woodcuts by Thomas Bewick and his School,* and *W.H. Pyne's Rustic Vignettes for Artists and Craftsmen,* both published by Dover Publications Inc. 1962 and 1977 respectively.

Fiducia Press and Kingsmead Press

publish and supply books on local and social history, poetry, music, transport and allied subjects. Current titles include:-

<u>Poetry</u> - *Manly Monodes,* £3; *Tracts from the Tracks,* £5. <u>Transport</u> - *The Glastonbury Canal,* £5; *The Parrett Navigation,* £4; *The Severn Tunnel* (h/bk), £19.95; *Great Railway Battles,* £9.95. <u>Music</u> - *The Dave Collett Blues,* £5; *Recollections of Jazz in Bristol,* £10. <u>Local</u> - *Fussells Ironworks, Mells,* £5; *The Gentle Giants* (Shire horses hauling timber), £3; *Recollections of Chew Magna,* £5; *Exploring the Smaller Towns of Somerset,* £6.95.
Just Published - *Views of Labour and Gold,* a reprint of a book on political and moral economy by William Barnes (1801-1886), the Dorset poet, priest and schoomaster, £10.

All the above may be ordered, post free, from Fiducia Press at 10 Fairfield Road, Bristol BS3 1LG. Special rates for multiple, society and trade orders. For our lists of single copy rare/out-of-print transport and local books, photographs and transparencies for disposal contact 4 Woodspring Avenue, Weston-super- Mare BS22 9RJ.